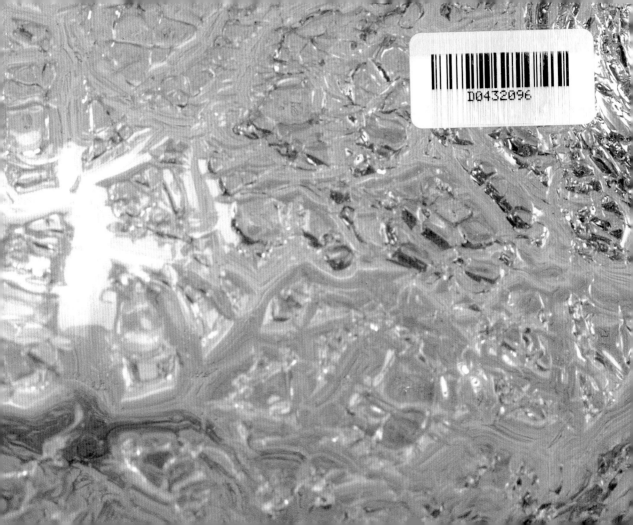

MURANO

poem BY Mark Doty

glass FROM THE J. Paul Getty Museum

LOS ANGELES

The Venetian island of Murano is an extraordinary place. At the mouth of the Adriatic, it served as a nexus between Europe and the Byzantine and Islamic worlds in the Middle Ages. The island's beauty led the local nobility to build luxurious palaces and gardens there. By the time of the Renaissance, Murano was known for its most famous product: *cristallo,* a colorless, transparent, and pure glass that resembled the rock crystal after which it was named. Craftsmen—Venetian locals as well as immigrants—developed innovative techniques to produce glorious colored, enameled, gilded, and engraved glass in refined and delicate forms. Murano glass became so famous, and so extraordinary, that the Venetian Senate decreed that no ordinary glass could be produced there.

A famous sixteenth-century metallurgist wrote that because of the fragility of glass, "one . . . must not give it too much love, and one must . . . understand it as an example of the life of man and of the things of this world, which, though beautiful, are transitory and frail." In like manner, Mark Doty's moving and contemplative poem uses Venice and its glass as a means of pondering human mortality and the mystery of artistic creation. It is, I think, worthy of its subjects.

CATHERINE HESS
ASSOCIATE CURATOR OF SCULPTURE

MURANO

Close my eyes and I'm a vessel. Make it
some lucent amphora, Venetian blue...

LYNDA HULL
"Rivers into Seas"

Toxic salts, arsenic and copper,
metal oxides firing the glassmaker's slag
to meteor lusters; sheet-glass

married to a hammered golden foil
then cut to bits: the gilt tiles
of the Byzantines—masters

brought to San Marco
to approximate, in jeweler's terms,
heaven—

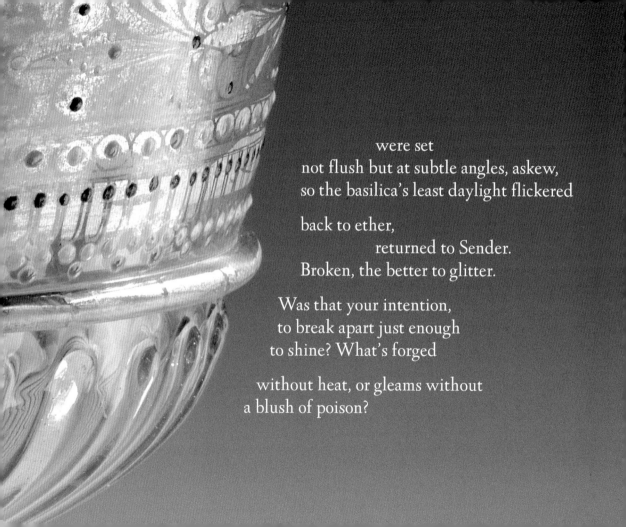

were set
not flush but at subtle angles, askew,
so the basilica's least daylight flickered

back to ether,
                        returned to Sender.
Broken, the better to glitter.

Was that your intention,
    to break apart just enough
to shine? What's forged

without heat, or gleams without
a blush of poison?

Outside Palazzo Grassi
—Fiat owns it now—upturned floodlamps
fire beneath the Grand Canal, so that light

through the stirred and ceaseless Adriatic
scrawls on ocher walls a rippling
suspiration:
      republic of instability,

                           in love
                               with reflection, made,
                                   in its every aspect,

                           to give back light.
                               To God?
                               I don't think so.

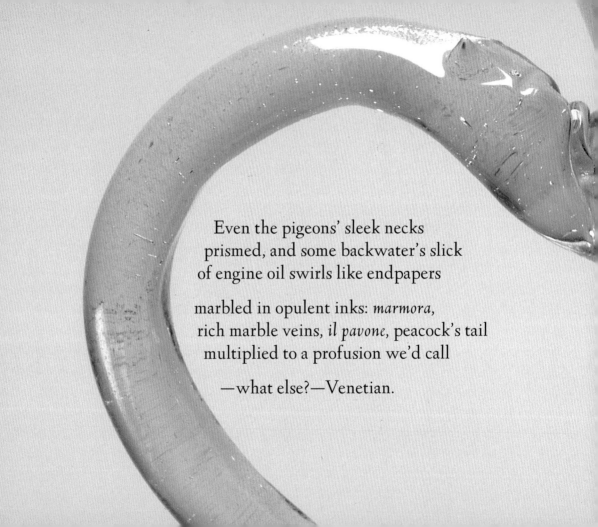

Even the pigeons' sleek necks
prismed, and some backwater's slick
of engine oil swirls like endpapers

marbled in opulent inks: *marmora*,
rich marble veins, *il pavone*, peacock's tail
multiplied to a profusion we'd call

—what else?—Venetian.

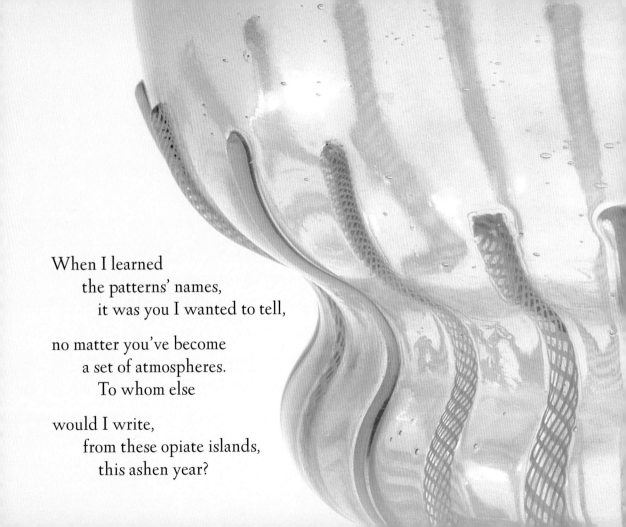

When I learned
    the patterns' names,
        it was you I wanted to tell,

no matter you've become
    a set of atmospheres.
        To whom else

would I write,
    from these opiate islands,
        this ashen year?

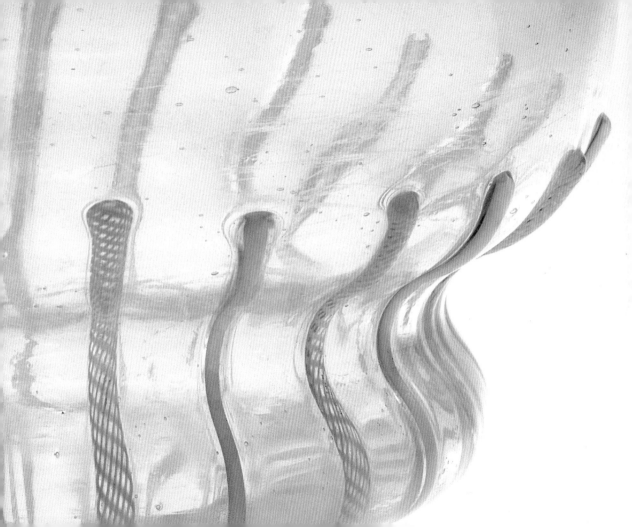

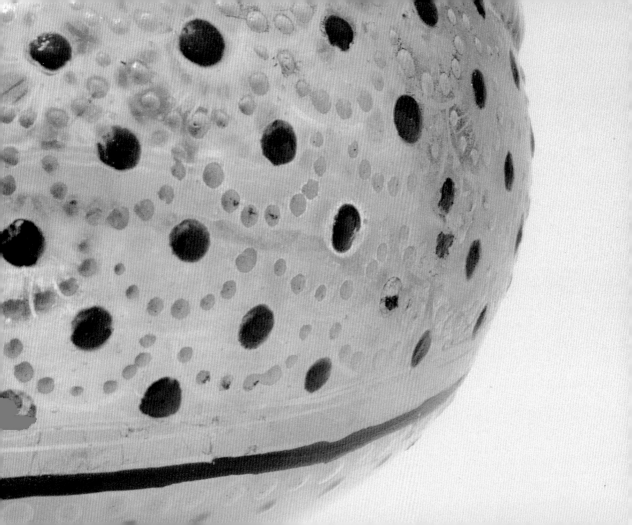

There's a Cornell box,
    in the Palazzo Venier, his version
      of a Byzantine vitrine:

ranks of little bottles,
    sealed and rowed
      on shelves before

the doubling mercury
    of a shiny American mirror.
      (Not one of those foggy

Venetian glasses; their mineral opacity
gives back, mostly, themselves—cloudy,
unlikely as their source. Is glass
this town's metaphor for itself?

Hallucinatory, fragile, dangerous:
distorting sulphurs and hazes,
dissolving palaces, molten appearances

on unstable ground.)
    Cornell's canopic jars
        preserve sands

and tinctures,
    volatile unguents,
        shreds of map and text.

One's a sealed vial
    of nothing
        but radiant gold;   only paint,
                treasure gathered
                  in the dimestores

        of Manhattan,
           but it doesn't matter;

this work —this *city* —

lives for the glamour
    we make of whatever's
     here. What's gold

but a physical
    species of joy?

        Venice is a world

of things he—and you—would cherish:
a jeweler's window Byzantine with marcasite,
a chilly galaxy you'd have worn,

its glitter restrained by the intimate alley
where jewelry's all that torches the dark.
Here's a clutch of Tintoretto silks, the sort

a girl in his turbulent air might bend to lift
as she hurries past the dim doorway of a room
where some miracle or martyrdom's occurring.

Here's another century's twilight
seeping between the columns,
winged lion, conquering saint,

portals of the dawn and evening
(which is which? in the Republic,
day began at sundown, a detail

you'd have liked),

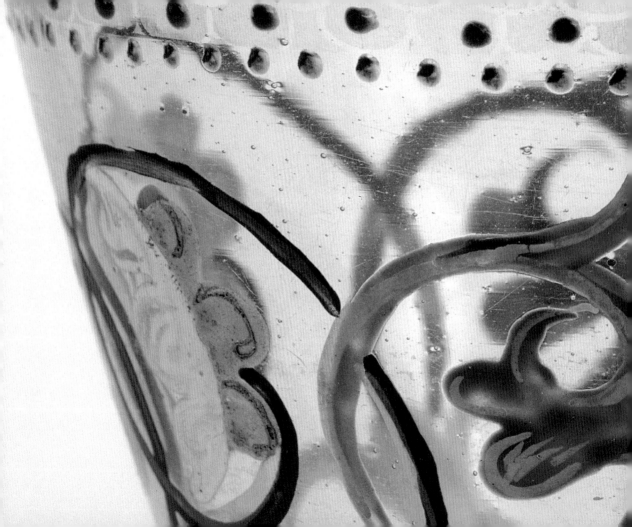

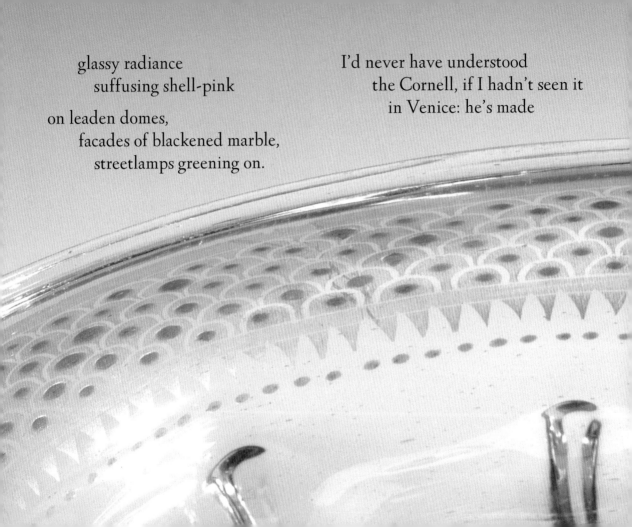

glassy radiance
  suffusing shell-pink

on leaden domes,
  facades of blackened marble,
  streetlamps greening on.

I'd never have understood
  the Cornell, if I hadn't seen it
  in Venice: he's made

this city's reliquary,
   perfect jewel-case to hold
     an empire's knucklebone,

scraps of its fabrics
   and foils, its sour essences,
     precious vapors and perfumes:

capital of the made, dear,
where the given's smoked
and polished, plucked

from the ovens'
chemical heats, beaten
and gilded to glory:

rotting palaces flung straight
up from the sea, yellow
of mummy wrappings,

coral and rose
  moldering now, faded
   to precisely these

bruised and mottled
  rusts; acid, lichenous
   greens: vitriolized,

encrusted, pearled.
  The city of artiface,
   darling, the city I love,

is a nightmare.
        Doesn't it smell
            of piss and dissolution,

isn't it glazed
        with its own whispers,
            this tide-licked,

self-absorbed, indifferent
        place? These mirrors
            reflect themselves,

not you. Is this
        what becomes of art,
            the hard-won permanence

outside of time? A struck
match-head of a city,
ungodly lonely

in its patina of fumes
and ash? Gorgeous scrap heap
where no one lives,

or hardly anyone.
Did you have to burn
so harshly bright?
Wasn't the world
ruin enough? Why
break yourself further
and faster?

This dock
rocks and pitches, no solid
place to stand, and
on the lagoon's surface
a red boat's flank is troubled
into jasper, foaming
furnace-sheen. A *vaporetto*

(hear, even in the word,
wild instability,
　　　　homage to mutable
airs and smokes?)
　　　　　　to Murano,

island of the glassmakers'
　　　exile. Wise city, to banish
　　　this business

　　　　　　　　　　　to its margins,
　　　　　　　　　　　　ancient ovens fired
　　　　　　　　　　　　all millennium

　　　　　　　　　　to incandescence.

Even a pouring, refracted city
    must protect itself.

Are you afraid,
    now you're salts and essences,
      the flung and gathered

elements from which any art
    is fused and blown?
      When were you ever

afraid to be spun out
    into some other order,
      alloyed with strange metals,

thinned, dosed
    with just enough
      to become radiant,

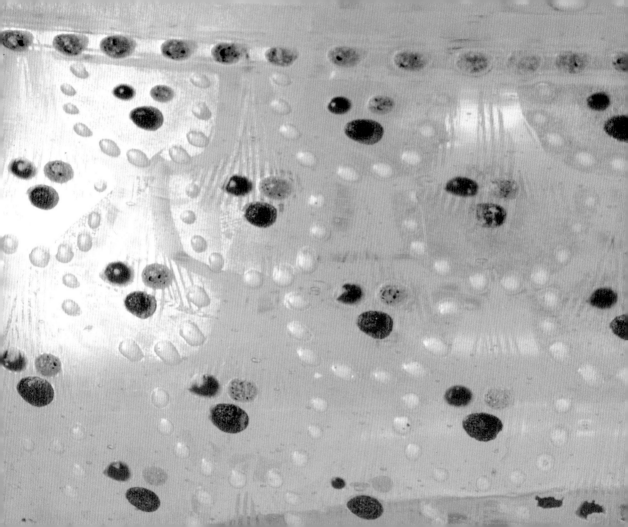

skin flushed with azure
    and a Pharaoh's wash of gold?
      Here the brilliant liquid

tormented into form,
    pincers and tongs,
    mouthpieces and pipes

to shape and set you
    spinning. Always
      the fate of the maker,

to become what's made
    —the gilt, permanent thing,
    of silk or sentences,

metal or silicas?
    Did I tell you I saw,
    on a dusty lower shelf

in the Treasury of San Marco,
    a pair of golden birds
      welded to a golden bough

complete with hammered leaves,
    some Grecian goldsmith's
      bright-beaked accomplishment

stolen from Byzantium?

And now you're glass.

Murano Glass from the Preceding Pages

Footed Bowl
(*Coppa*)
Italian (Murano)
ca. 1500
H: 4⅞ in.
84.DK.660

Ice-Glass Situla
(*Secchiello*)
Italian (Murano)
or *façon de Venise*,
the Netherlands
1550–1600
H: 4 in.
84.DK.657

Wineglass
Italian (Murano)
or *façon de Venise*
(Tuscany)
1600–50
H: 5⅞ in.
84.DK.541

Goblet
Italian (Murano)
ca. 1500
H: 7¹⁄₁₆ in.
84.DK.534

Goblet
Italian (Murano)
1475–1500
H: 7⁵⁄₁₆ in.
84.DK.533

FOOTED BOWL
(*COPPA*)
Italian (Murano)
ca. 1500
H: 7 in.
84.DK.535

PILGRIM FLASK
Italian (Murano)
Late fifteenth or
early sixteenth
century
H: 14 ¹³⁄₁₆ in.
84.DK.538

FOOTED BOWL
(*COPPA*)
Italian (Murano)
Early sixteenth
century
H: 9 ½ in.
84.DK.511

EWER
Italian (Murano)
Late fifteenth or
early sixteenth
century
H: 10 ¹¹⁄₁₆ in.
84.DK.512

Double-Handled
Filigrana Vase
Italian (Murano?)
or *façon de Venise*
(possibly northern
Europe)
1550–70
H: 8 7/8 in.
84.DK.654

Filigrana Umbo Vase
Italian
(probably Murano)
1580–1600
H: 8 1/3 in.
84.DK.656

Filigrana Bottle
(*Kuttrolf*)
Italian (Murano)
Late sixteenth or
early seventeenth
century
H: 9 3/8 in.
84.DK.661

Goblet
Italian (Murano)
Late fifteenth or
early sixteenth
century
H: 5 7/16 in.
84.DK.540

BOWL
Italian (Murano)
Early sixteenth
century
H: 1 ¾ in.
DIAM: 12 in.
84.DK.536

STEMMED *FILIGRANA*
WINEGLASS (*TAZZA*)
Italian
(probably Murano)
Late sixteenth to
early seventeenth
century
H: 4 ¼ in.
84.DK.652

PILGRIM FLASK
Italian (Murano)
1500–20
H: 12 ⁵⁄₁₆ in.
84.DK.539

FOOTED BOWL
WITH PAPAL ARMS
(*COPPA*)
Italian (Murano)
1513–34
H: 6 ⁵⁄₁₆ in.
84.DK.655

© 2000 The J. Paul Getty Trust
1200 Getty Center Drive
Suite 400
Los Angeles, CA 90049-1681

www.getty.edu/publications

AT THE J. PAUL GETTY MUSEUM:
Christopher Hudson, Publisher
Mark Greenberg, Managing Editor

PROJECT STAFF:
John Harris, Editor
Kurt Hauser, Designer
Amita Molloy, Production Coordinator
Jack Ross, Photographer

PRINTED IN Hong Kong

COVER: FOOTED BOWL (*COPPA*), ca. 1500 (detail). Los Angeles, J. Paul Getty Museum, 84.DK.660.

P. 5: Giovanni Maria Butteri (Italian, 1540–ca. 1606). *The Medici Glass Workshop* (detail), 1570. Florence, Palazzo Vecchio, Studiolo of Francesco I. Photo: Scala, Milan.

"Murano" from *Sweet Machine* by Mark Doty. Copyright © 1998 by Mark Doty. Reprinted by permission of HarperCollins Publishers, Inc.

Library of Congress Cataloging-in-Publication Data
Doty, Mark
   Murano : poem / by Mark Doty ; glass from the J. Paul Getty Museum
     p. cm.
   ISBN 0-89236-598-6
     1. Glass art—Italy—Murano—Poetry. 2. Murano (Italy)—Poetry. I. J. Paul Getty Museum. II. Title.

PS3554.O798 M8 2000
811'.54—dc21

                                      00-022399

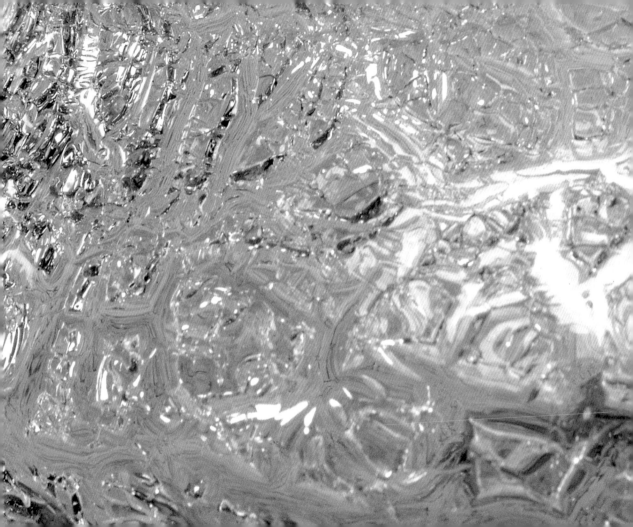